First World War
and Army of Occupation
War Diary
France, Belgium and Germany

41 DIVISION
Headquarters, Branches and Services
Royal Army Ordnance Corps
Deputy Assistant Director Ordnance Services
1 March 1918 - 30 November 1919

WO95/2624/4

The Naval & Military Press Ltd
www.nmarchive.com
Published in association with The National Archives

Published by

The Naval & Military Press Ltd

Unit 10 Ridgewood Industrial Park,

Uckfield, East Sussex,

TN22 5QE England

Tel: +44 (0) 1825 749494

www.naval-military-press.com

www.nmarchive.com

Contents

Document type	Place/Title	Date From	Date To
Heading	WO95/2624/4		
War Diary	Camposampiero	01/03/1918	01/03/1918
War Diary	Courtrelle	05/03/1918	05/03/1918
War Diary	Coullemont	06/03/1918	09/03/1918
War Diary	Lucheux	10/03/1918	20/03/1918
War Diary	Baisieux	21/03/1918	26/03/1918
War Diary	Doullens	27/03/1918	29/03/1918
War Diary	St. Amand	30/03/1918	03/04/1918
War Diary	Steenvorde	04/04/1918	09/04/1918
War Diary	Dirty Bucket Camp Nr Vlamertinghe	10/04/1918	14/04/1918
War Diary	Elms School-Nr Poperinghe	15/04/1918	29/04/1918
War Diary	Lovie	30/04/1918	30/04/1918
War Diary	La Lovie (nr Poperinghe)	02/05/1918	31/05/1918
War Diary	La Lovie	01/06/1918	02/06/1918
War Diary	Nieurlet	04/06/1918	06/06/1918
War Diary	Eperlecques	07/06/1918	25/06/1918
War Diary	Oudezeele	26/06/1918	01/07/1918
War Diary	Abeele Aerodrome	02/07/1918	28/08/1918
War Diary	Wizernes	29/08/1918	01/09/1918
War Diary	Nr Abeele Hillhoek	03/09/1918	28/09/1918
War Diary	Mersey Cross Busseboom	29/09/1918	16/10/1918
War Diary	Daddizeele	17/10/1918	19/10/1918
War Diary	Poeselhoek Nr. Gullighem	22/10/1918	25/10/1918
War Diary	Hooghe	27/10/1918	31/10/1918
War Diary	T'Hooghe	01/11/1918	02/11/1918
War Diary	St. Louis	03/11/1918	05/11/1918
War Diary	Vichte	07/11/1918	10/11/1918
War Diary	Niederbrakel	14/11/1918	17/11/1918
War Diary	Sant Bergen	18/11/1918	19/11/1918
War Diary	Grammont	21/11/1918	14/12/1918
War Diary	Braine L'Alleud	17/12/1918	19/12/1918
War Diary	Vinalmont	20/12/1918	12/01/1919
War Diary	Wahn	13/01/1919	29/01/1919
War Diary	Deutz	30/01/1919	02/03/1919
War Diary	Germany	01/03/1919	01/03/1919
War Diary	Deutz	01/03/1919	31/03/1919
War Diary	Coln Deutz	01/04/1919	30/04/1919
War Diary	Deutz	01/05/1919	31/10/1919
War Diary	Deutz Koln.	01/11/1919	08/11/1919
War Diary	Deutz	09/11/1919	30/11/1919

17 DADOS 41st Divn

Instructions regarding War Diaries and Intelligence Summaries are contained in F. S. Regs., Part II. and the Staff Manual respectively. Title pages will be prepared in manuscript.

WAR DIARY
or
~~INTELLIGENCE SUMMARY.~~
(Erase heading not required.)

March 1918 (Sheet 1)

Army Form C. 2118.

23

Place	Date	Hour	Summary of Events and Information	Remarks and references to Appendices
	March	1918		
CAMPOSAMPIERO	1	March	Entrained for FRANCE, taking large amount of clean clothes for Baths as well as gas helmets & normal Ordce stores	
COURTRELLE	5	March	Arrived at MONDICOURT this morning. Allotted dump in farm here but found road too bad for lorry work & changed next day to	
COULLEMONT	6	March	COULLEMONT about 2 kilos from DHQ	
	7	"	ADOS IV Corps called. Railhead will be FREVENT	
	8	"	DHQ moved to LUCHEUX about 6 kilos. away & want me to move	
	9	"	Spent rest of morning trying to find new dump at LUCHEUX. Arranged to move dump to a mill, & office to farm some 200 yds away	
LUCHEUX	10	"	Moved to this place. Saw Staff Captn 123 Bde as to sorting stores to units & rode over to HQ 122 Bde. as to same purpose.	
	11		Went to 124 Bde at SOUS ST LEGER. 32 RF, 21 KRR, 11 RW Kents are to be disbanded	
	12		Went to RA HQ at GRANICOURT. The 3 Battn Bde is to be adopted; so 11 RW Kents, 32 RF, 21 KRR will be disbanded	
	13		Went to IV Corps HQ, saw ADOS & to HQ 25th, 6th, 51st Divns	
	16		Went to GRANICOURT (RA HQ) & met I.O.M who came to inspect the guns. Divl Conference in evening. Stores though arrived have not yet materialised as trucks have not come	
	17		Disbanded units of 122 & 124 Bdes returning Mob. Equipment. The 4 MG Coys are to form a Divl Battn from today	

T2134. Wt. W708—776. 500000. 4/15. Sir J. C. & S.

Instructions regarding War Diaries and Intelligence Summaries are contained in F. S. Regs., Part II. and the Staff Manual respectively. Title pages will be prepared in manuscript.

DADOS 41 Div

WAR DIARY or ~~INTELLIGENCE SUMMARY.~~

(Erase heading not required.)

March 1918 (Sheet 2)

Army Form C. 2118.

Place	Date	Hour	Summary of Events and Information	Remarks and references to Appendices
LUCHEUX	18	March	Went to 123 and 124 Inf Bdes in afternoon. Disbanded units have returned stores pretty satisfactorily	
	20	March	Issued Lewis guns for AA to Battalions, Bdes of RFA, & DAC.	
BAISIEUX	21	March	Division moved here. German attack on big front has just begun. Have got a fair store	
	22	March	Division ordered forward. I remain here pending further orders	
	24	March	Went to DHQ having picked up 25 Lewis guns, found them moving back. I took guns to Bde transport who were loaded & would not receive, went back to DHQ & finally got orders to bring them back here & await events. I am now overloaded with stores recently received which units cannot take & I cannot get reconsigned, & am in a quandary as to dealing with them, especially as communication is so exceedingly difficult	
	25	March	ALBERT reported to be evacuated, or on the point of being so. No news of any certain value & no orders have come through	
	26	March	Received order to move to DOULLENS. Started lorries off with stores to go to & fro till everything (including Baths, Officers kit & Div! Stores) removed.	
DOULLENS	27	March	Cannot find out where DHQ are. Lorries still going day & night. DAQMG came in afternoon.	
	28	March	Got everything satisfactorily from BAISIEUX. All have worked splendidly. Got sanction of DDOS 3rd Army to draw 500 Box Respirators as none have come from Base.	
	29	March	Moved myself with small staff to DHQ at ST AMANDS. Took some RO. Sponges for RA. to SOUASTRE in route & m.g. belts for MG Bttn	
ST. AMANDS	30 } 31 }	March	Have got some stores brought up & started distributing from here. Units are in a bad way. Large losses of Lewis & machine guns, packs, gt. Coats & Equipment.	

31/3/18 H Sprange[?] Major DADOS. 41 Div

D.A.D.O.S. No. ... 5 - APR 1918

T2134. Wt. W708—776. 500000. 4/15. Sir J. C. & S.

Instructions regarding War Diaries and Intelligence Summaries are contained in F. S. Regs., Part II. and the Staff Manual respectively. Title pages will be prepared in manuscript.

7

DADOS
4 Div[n].

WAR DIARY
or
~~INTELLIGENCE SUMMARY.~~
(Erase heading not required.)

APRIL 1918
(Sheet 1)

Army Form C. 2118.

Place	Date	Hour	Summary of Events and Information	Remarks and references to Appendices
ST AMANDS	April	1 & 2	Have managed to fix up RA. (who will stay when we leave & pass to 37th Div) fairly well to meet pressing needs.	
	April	3.	Proceeded from ST AMANDS via HESDIN to BOULOGNE – DOULLENS stores are [illegible] route in trucks, & personnel in lorries	
STEENVOORDE	April	4	Went to CALAIS & arranged about "refit" demands. Moved to STEENVOORDE. We are now in Second Army & VIII Corps.	
	April	5	Went to 122 Inf Bde, ADOS VIII Corps, Gun Pk No 2 & 124 Inf Bde.	
	April	6	All the Lewis guns & Stokes Mortars demanded last night came to day. M.G. Battns have some surplus guns	
	April	7.	Trucks from DOULLENS & stores from CALAIS which meet my indents practically in full for clothing &c, arrived to day. Whole day & extra lorries required to draw them from railhead	
	April	8 & 9	Units on the move: this makes it impossible for them to come to draw stores, and will leave them too far off for transport to [illegible]. Sent out as much as I could	
Dirty Bucket Camp nr. VLAMERTINGHE	April	10	Moved to this Camp. All day taken in moving stores forward	
	April	11 & 12	A lot of stores have come in the clothing line & units as a whole are fairly well equipped in that respect. ADOS VIII Corps	
	April	13	There is a difficulty apparently about getting limbered wagons from Base, as none have yet come to replace losses	
	April	14	Apparently we are now under IInd in place of VIII Corps. Received orders to move to-morrow to Camp nr. POPERINGHE, & accordingly had stores from railhead taken there direct. Have cleared dump here pretty well & are mobile at this end	
ELMS School nr POPERINGHE	April	16.	Moved this morning. Hope units will come in to clear the bulk stores which came yesterday	
	April	17	Stores coming up well & things running pretty smoothly	
	April	18	Walked to II. Corps & saw ADOS. CALAIS want to cancel indents up to 13th: ADOS arranged with CALAIS that those named by me should stand	
	April	20	Limbered wagon shortage nearly made up. Bicycles now the chief deficit. Have cancelled all pre-31 March indents, & given CALAIS list of subsequent ones which are to stand though before 13 April in date	
	April	23	Have collected & issued 4 more Lewis guns to Tank Btn.	

T2134. Wt. W708–776. 500000. 4/15. Sir J. C. & S.

Instructions regarding War Diaries and Intelligence Summaries are contained in F. S. Regs., Part II. and the Staff Manual respectively. Title pages will be prepared in manuscript.

DADOS. 41 Divn.

WAR DIARY
or
~~INTELLIGENCE SUMMARY.~~
(Erase heading not required.)

April 1918 (Sheet 2)

Army Form C. 2118.

Place	Date	Hour	Summary of Events and Information	Remarks and references to Appendices
ELMS SCHOOL to POPERINGHE	April 26		Q.M. Meeting to-day. General complaint as to extra stores not being accompanied by additions to transport. Divn. HQ returned to this place	
	April 27		Went to Divl. Train & M.T. Coy. Winter clothing is to be sent on to me	
	April 29		DHQ moved to LOVIE Chateau. Proven railhead badly shelled, stores (58 trucks) sent to ROUSBRUGGE - HARINGHE	
LOVIE	April 30		Moved here to-day. Luckily no stores came up as railhead is ST. OMER! Units lately have been drawing badly & not coming in. This makes me very trouble	
			Sparges Major DADOS 41 Divn. 30/4/1918	

T2134. Wt. W708—776. 500000. 4/15. Sir J. C. & S.

Instructions regarding War Diaries and Intelligence Summaries are contained in F. S. Regs., Part II. and the Staff Manual respectively. Title pages will be prepared in manuscript.

DADOS 41st Divn

WAR DIARY or ~~INTELLIGENCE SUMMARY.~~

(Erase heading not required.)

May 1918

Army Form C. 2118.

Vol 24

Place	Date	Hour	Summary of Events and Information	Remarks and references to Appendices
La Lovie	May	2	Stores coming up but Railhead changed to St OMER these last 2 days has made drawing impossible. Am getting stores to new Railhead at Rousbrugge	
(Poperinghe)	May	3	Demanded 18pdr. for 13th Bty	
	May	4	4.5 How carriage demanded for 17th Bty. Divl Conference	
	May	5	Had to send all the way to WATTEN to fetch 18pdr for No 2 Gun Park	
	May	6	4.5 How ready at No 2 G.P. Asked ADOS if we shall have to send. it is too far for horses – & hook the carriage to our lorry on this occasion. He told me to leave G.P. to do it	
	May	10	Q.M. Meeting. No complaints except shortage of Mess tin covers & brush cases. Bicycles are now practically complete	
	May	11	Base have constantly duplicated issues lately, which makes things difficult & complicates accounts.	
	May	13	The 29th D.A. are returning to their own Divn & 41st D.A. coming back to us in a few days	
	May	15	41st D.A. returned, & 29th ADC attached to me left yesterday	
	May	17	Q.M. Conference. Saw H.Q. D.A. as to their position as regards stores.	
	May	18	Went round Bdes in afternoon. Saw OC Divl Bks as to summer underclothes	
	May	19	Conference with ADOS at II Corps as to new lateral issue of stores proposal	
	May	21	Went to ST OMER, & II Corps en route	
	May	23	Establt of Lewis guns, is now to be 32 + AA guns. Indented for 4 more, which will give Battns (4×9) 24 + 4 (?)	
	May	24	Q.M. Conference. Lt. Elliott ADOS arrived this evening for 1 month's course.	
	May	27	Visited 190 Bde R.F.A. wagon lines. A.I.A. called & inspected Armourers shop	
	May	29	Sent lorry for 2 remaining Stokes Mortars which will give RA T.M. Btys their full establt (12)	ADOS II Corps called
	May	31	Q.M. Meeting. All Q.M.s agreed as to existing superfluity of equipment in various items under Mob. Table. Visited units.	

31. V. 1918 [signature] Major DADOS 41 Divn

6

DADOS

41 Division

Instructions regarding War Diaries and Intelligence Summaries are contained in F. S. Regs., Part II. and the Staff Manual respectively. Title pages will be prepared in manuscript.

WAR DIARY
or
INTELLIGENCE SUMMARY.
(Erase heading not required.)

June 1918

Army Form C. 2118.

Vol 26

Place	Date	Hour	Summary of Events and Information	Remarks and references to Appendices
	June 1918			
LA LOVIE	1	-	Went to Corps & saw ADOS, with DAQMG. Stopped issues from Base for present as we are going to move out	
	2		Inspected new pattern of MG Belt boxes for expendable belts at MG Battn HQ	
NIEURLET	4		Moved here to-day - now being in XXII Corps. Called at II Corps en route	
	5	-	Went to 22 Corps but found them moving - Divn now apparently in VII Corps. Also to HQ 124 Inf Bde. In afternoon went to HQ Second Army & saw DDOS	
	6		Went to EPERLECQUES to find suitable dump &c & HQ 39 Divn. Lt. ELLIOTT relinquished to BOULOGNE	
EPERLECQUES	7		Moved to EPERLECQUES. Went to HQ 123 Inf Bde. ADOS VII Corps called, but I was out	
	9.		Went to 15 Hants. 18 KRR. HQ 122 Inf Bde & in afternoon HQ 41st DA.	
	10.		Went to CALAIS with DAQMG & SC 124 Inf Bde & were taken over stores, Salvage, & Workshops	
	11		Went to HQ 41st DA	
	12		Went to VII Corps (ADOS out), 18 KRR, Gun Park No 2, HQ 122 Inf Bde	
	13		Went to VII Corps & saw ADOS, & indented for 6 "Scholastic" Trench Mortars for RA	
	15		Went to HQ DA as to mortars. Visited O.C. 12th E Surrey, IMs for instruction	
	16		ADOS came in afternoon. Army sent letter [illegible] as to issuing	
	19		Went to WATTEN (VII Corps). Reception Camp now started near Divl [illegible]. Went there & find that hundreds of men are in a [illegible] & [illegible] state	[illegible]
	20		After much haversing, the RA have got their 6 "brick" mortars	
	21		QM Meeting. Went to 18 KRR & HQ 122 Bde	
	22		Went to VIII Corps & saw ADOS	
	24		Went to Divl Reception Camp, to RW Kent, & Sherwoods battn. ADOS called. Suspended stores from Base.	
	25		Divn will now move back to Flanders, taking over from French	
OUDEZEELE	26		Moved to OUDEZEELE this morning. Wired Base to send stores - Went to HQ DA.	
	27		Went to ESQUELBECQ - this is to be railhead, from which supplies can be moved by metre gauge line	
	29		Went to STEENVOORDE, 12 E Surrey, Divl Ammn Dump, HQ 122 Bde - We now come under XIX Corps	
	30		ADOS XIX Corps called. Delivered 6 Trench Mortars to RA TM Bde. Incoming stores taken to new dump at aerodrome near ABEELE.	

30. VI. 1918

[signature] Major
DADOS 41 Div

T2134. Wt. W708—776. 500000. 4/15. Sir J. C. & S.

Instructions regarding War Diaries and Intelligence Summaries are contained in F. S. Regs., Part II. and the Staff Manual respectively. Title pages will be prepared in manuscript.

DADOS 41 Divn

WAR DIARY
or
~~INTELLIGENCE SUMMARY.~~
(Erase heading not required.)

July 1918

Army Form C. 2118.

VR 27

Place	Date	Hour	Summary of Events and Information	Remarks and references to Appendices
OUDEZEELE	1 July	1918	Went to ADOS. XIX Corps, & Divl. Armr. Dump with DAQMG, also Armr. Railhead.	
ABEELE	2 July	–	Moved to ABEELE aerodrome. Went to XIX Corps ADOS, & 138 F.A. (Divl. Rest station)	
AERODROME	4 July	–	Visited Train HQ & Train & Infantry Wagon lines	
	5 July	.	ADOS visited. SC 123 Bde called	
	6 July	–	Visited 11 Queens. QM meeting in morning	
	9 July	.	Went to Reception Camp with DAQMG. They will move shortly & come probably fairly close to railhead	
	11 July	–	Received 4 Lewis guns for each Field Coy under new establt.	
	12 July	.	QM. Meeting	
	13 July	.	Fetched 6 sub-beds for Stokes Mortars & delivered to Divl. TMO. This completes the RA	
	15 July	.	Went to see S.S.O. as to method for drive to supply to aeroplanes	
	16 July		Visited 26 R.F. Divl. Reception Camp is shortly moving to near BOLLEZEELE, which will be a slight improvement. Stores are difficult to get away from ESQUELBECQUES under French control and frequently can't be drawn till well on in the afternoon.	
	18 July		The long sought racks for Lewis guns arrived for sample to-day. They are very simple & easily made, which makes delay in supply inexplicable	
	19 July		Went to ST. OMER to buy leather. QM. Conference in afternoon. Visited D/187	
	21 July		ADOS attended trial of Lewis gun racks in limber packed as suggested in QMG's circular letter with 4 guns &c. per ½ limber	
	23 July		Went with DAQMG & saw Salvage Officer. also to Corps Conference with DAAG as to transport &c. in event of moving rapidly	
	25 July		Visited all Train Coys to look at shop working. ADOS came.	
	26 July		Q.M. Meeting. General complaints of the QMs as to the Reception Camp. & state of troops sent back therefrom.	
	27 July		Had an inspection of alternative ways of loading limbered wagons with Lewis guns, magazines &c. at Divl. HQ. More magazines & less S.A.A. seemed to be generally preferred	
	29 July		Visited HQ & No. 4 Coy Train.	
	30 July		Visited 122 Bde Billet Camp. Guns & Hows are being replaced very quickly nowadays.	

31/VII/1918 — [signature] Major, DADOS 41 Divn

T2134. Wt. W708—776. 500000. 4/15. Sir J. C. & S.

Instructions regarding War Diaries and Intelligence Summaries are contained in F. S. Regs., Part II. and the Staff Manual respectively. Title pages will be prepared in manuscript.

DADOS 41st Div'n

WAR DIARY
or
~~INTELLIGENCE SUMMARY.~~
(Erase heading not required.)

August 1918

Army Form C. 2118.

Vol 28

Place	Date	Hour	Summary of Events and Information	Remarks and references to Appendices
	August 1918			
ABEELE AERODROME	Aug	1	ADOS called. Visited 15 Hants as to their being supplied by lorry when they move to WIZERNES area [illegible]	
	Aug	2	DOS [illegible] with DDOS Second Army & ADOS XV Corps. Cdr Dawson went on leave.	
	Aug	3	Salvage Officer called. [illegible] to Salvage Dump to arrange regular collection of [illegible] stores. S/C Stacey [illegible] Chief Clerk	
	Aug	4	S.M.O. [illegible] as [illegible] & ADOS called	
	Aug	[illegible]	Went to Salvage Dump. RA [illegible] artificers [illegible] for instruction [illegible] guns	
	Aug	8	Went on leave to England	
	Aug	12	Sub Cdr WHITE arrived from 30th Div'n. Sub Cdr RICHARDSON going there in his place	
	Aug	18	5 American Mechanics came for weeks instruction in Div'l Armourers shop. Lt. F.L. HUTH AOD arrived on a month's course	
	Aug	27	Returned from leave. Div'l Artillery moved for Bde purposes to 34th Div'n. Issue of stores stopped as Div'n to about to move	
	Aug	28.	Lorries left for WIZERNES to find a suitable dump, taking stores left & reserve stores.	
WIZERNES	Aug	29	Div'n (less R.A. [illegible] 34th Div'n) moved to WIZERNES [illegible]	
			[illegible] same place	
	Aug	[illegible]	[illegible] ADOS XV Corps [illegible]	
	Aug	31	[illegible] LUMBRES [illegible]	

[illegible] Major
DADOS 41 Div'n
31/8/1918

T2134. Wt. W708—776. 500000. 4/15. Sir J. C. & S.

9

Instructions regarding War Diaries and Intelligence Summaries are contained in F. S. Regs., Part II. and the Staff Manual respectively. Title pages will be prepared in manuscript.

DADOS 41 Div

WAR DIARY
or
~~INTELLIGENCE~~ SUMMARY.
(*Erase heading not required.*)

~~AUG~~ DADOS 41 D SEPTEMBER 1918

Army Form C. 2118.

Sheet 1

29

Place	Date	Hour	Summary of Events and Information	Remarks and references to Appendices
WIZERNES	Sept	1	Div ordered back to line. 122nd Bde to go to day, 123 to morrow. 124 has never left line. Stopped stores on [illegible]	
ABEELE HILLHOEK	Sept	3	Moved to Sheet 27 K 18 c 9 7 late dump of 27th American Div. Recognised stores which arrived at LUMBRES [illegible] to rail[head] which will be [illegible] on Sept 5th. Took over gum boots, leather [illegible] & [illegible] stands from 27th Am. Div.	
	Sept	5	[illegible] Went to DADOS 34 Div. Placed [illegible] back from 34th Div. Order	
	Sept	7	ADOS brought American cloth for AA [illegible] to be put on [illegible]	
	Sept	8	DADOS 34 Div. Came to [illegible] at [illegible]. Railhead now at [illegible]	
	Sept	9	Went to Ration dump. [illegible] of QMs. Visited HQ 123 Bde, 12 E Surrey, 18 KRR, MG Btn. Went with DADMG to consider site of new dump & to No 2 [illegible].	Went for 1 blanket per man
	Sept	11	[illegible]	
	Sept	12	[illegible] HQ 123 & 124 Inf Bdes	
	Sept	13	[illegible] Saw ADOS at advanced Ordce Dump at [illegible]	
	Sept	14	Saw ADTS as to gas clothing. ADOS called after lunch	
	Sept	15	Went to Railhead. Went over Div Salvage Dump. To 138 FA & 123 Bde HQ. Spoke to S.C. 123rd Bde as to [illegible] heavy clothing	[illegible]
	Sept	16	[illegible]. Sent blankets [illegible] to 124 Inf Bde [illegible]. Blankets (1st) now issued to all units	
	Sept	17	[illegible] to HQ 123 Bde & QMs stores of units in this Bde. Gum boots have now been distributed	
	Sept	18	Went to No 11 & 12 [illegible] Workshops	
	Sept	19	Went to A/190 [illegible]	
	Sept	20	[illegible] for [illegible] American Canvas	
	Sept	21	Went [illegible] Salvage Dump [illegible]. ADOS called	
	Sept	22	Staff Conference in morning. [illegible] nearly all distributed now to units concerned	
	Sept	23	Went to [illegible] & [illegible] to the other 50 [illegible]	
	Sept	24	Went to [illegible] & Railhead. ADOS called	
	Sept	25	Went to [illegible] DADOS 34 Div came. Went to 41st Reception Camp.	
	Sept	26	Went to Salvage Dump & MG Batt. 124th Inf Bde returning to day	

T2134. Wt. W708—776. 500000. 4/15. Sir J. C. & S.

Instructions regarding War Diaries and Intelligence Summaries are contained in F. S. Regs., Part II. and the Staff Manual respectively. Title pages will be prepared in manuscript.

DADOS.
41 Div.

WAR DIARY
or
~~INTELLIGENCE SUMMARY.~~
(Erase heading not required.)

Sept. 1918. (Sheet 2)

Army Form C. 2118.

Place	Date	Hour	Summary of Events and Information	Remarks and references to Appendices
HILLHOEK nr. ABEELE	Sept.	27	Went to Reception Camp & 122 HQ. DHQ. moving forward to-day. I remain here.	
	Sept	28.	Attack began to-day on Second Army front. Went to Gun Park in morning & DHQ in afternoon.	
MERSEY CROSS	Sept.	29.	Moved to Mersey Cross. Busseboom to-day as was DHQ. ADOS. called. Stores are beginning to accumulate & units are unable to draw. Battle going well. big advance	
BUSSEBOOM	Sept.	30.	Sent up 300 L.G. magazines to SAA section. No Vickers guns lost yet (apparently no Lewis	

30/IX/1918

E. Spranger Major
DADOS 41 Div.

Instructions regarding War Diaries and Intelligence Summaries are contained in F. S. Regs., Part II. and the Staff Manual respectively. Title Pages will be prepared in manuscript.

DADOS. 41st Div[n] 26

WAR DIARY
or
INTELLIGENCE SUMMARY
(Erase heading not required.)

Army Form C. 2118

October 1918 (Sheet 1)

Vol 30

Place	Date October	Hour	Summary of Events and Information	Remarks and references to Appendices
MERSEY Cross	1		Rode to DHQ at LANKHOF Farm. ADOS called. DHQ likely to move forward, while we stop	
BUSSEBOOM	2		Went to Reception Camp. Some QMs called. Only 2 Lewis guns yet issued	
	3		Went to [illegible] Farm, [illegible] [illegible] [illegible] have kindly left all their [illegible] for DADOS to remove [illegible] B Echelon 124 Bde. Units will want boots badly	
	4		AA&QMG & ADOS called. Sent 30 Lewis guns to 122nd (18) & 123rd (12) Bde. D.HQ moving to near GHELUVELT. Wired for leave to demand boots [illegible]	
	5		Went to [illegible] [illegible] [illegible]. ADOS called twice. Wired for boot [illegible].	
	6		Thousands of [illegible] & drawers came [illegible] not yet expected. Went to DHQ	
	7		Visited all 3 Bns of 122 Bde & HQ 122. Bde is now at [illegible] [illegible] [illegible]	
	8		ADOS, AA&QMG called. Visited HQ 122, HQ 124 Bdes, 10 Queens	
	9		Went to HQ 122 & [illegible] [illegible] of all Bde [illegible]. Visited 15 Hants, 12 E Surreys & HQ 122 & 124 Bde	
	11		Sent all lorries to [illegible] to bring back [illegible] [illegible]	
	12.		Went to Railhead & XIX Corps Troops. ADOS called & brought Special slips.	
	13		Went to DHQ. Div[n] has advanced. Losses slight	
	15		Residue of vests & drawers came. ADOS called. Lieut HUTH left for tempy duty with 36 Div[n]	
	16		Went to DHQ who move forward to morrow, & to DADIZEELE to try to find a dump. Am to have an advanced Dump there. Stopped stores from Base	
DADIZEELE	17.		Moved to DADIZEELE. Fetching stores up gradually - a long way on bad road.	
	18		Wired Base to send clothing, boots, nose bags &c already demanded & stopped by wire of 16th.	
	19.		Decided to take all stores & wired Base accordingly. Went to DHQ.	
PORSELHOEK nr GULLEGHEM	22.		Moved here to day. Stores were fairly well cleared by units in last 3 days. Went to XIX Corps Tr. Rootb but ADOS out	

1875 Wt. W593/826 1,000,000 4/15 J.B.C. & A. A.D.S.S./Forms/C. 2118.

Army Form C. 2118.

Instructions regarding War Diaries and Intelligence Summaries are contained in F. S. Regs., Part II. and the Staff Manual respectively. Title Pages will be prepared in manuscript.

DADOS.
41 Divⁿ

WAR DIARY
or
~~INTELLIGENCE SUMMARY~~
(Erase heading not required.)

October 1918 (Sheet 2)

Place	Date	Hour	Summary of Events and Information	Remarks and references to Appendices
	Oct	23	Clothing & boots arrived at LEDEGHEM – fortunately new Railhead instead of TROIS ROIS, rails back	
	Oct.	24	Went to D.H.Q. 7500 Jerkins arrived: this should cover present strength of Div.	
	Oct.	25.	Went to D.H.Q. Clothing state again O.K.: this should keep things going satisfactorily.	
HOOGHE	Oct.	27.	Moved to HOOGHE – just outside of COURTRAI	
	Oct.	29	Went to 123 Bde. H.Q. Mysterious wire from Army as to alleged complaints about boots	
	Oct.	30.	Saw Staff Capt. 124 Bde. Large indents for all sorts of equipment from Inf. units	
	Oct.	31.	Went to No. 9 O.M. Workshops – R.A. H.Q. & saw S. Capt. as to carriage of C/187 apparently handed in weeks ago, but not repaired or replaced	

F. C. Spranger Major
DADOS 41 Divⁿ

31/X/1918

2449 Wt. W14957/M90 750,000 1/16 J.B.C. & A. Forms/C.2118/12.

DADOS 4 Div^n

Instructions regarding War Diaries and Intelligence Summaries are contained in F. S. Regs., Part II. and the Staff Manual respectively. Title Pages will be prepared in manuscript.

WAR DIARY
~~or~~
~~INTELLIGENCE SUMMARY~~
(Erase heading not required.)

Army Form C. 2118.

November 1918

Sheet 1

Place	Date	Hour	Summary of Events and Information	Remarks and references to Appendices
	November			
T'HOOGHE	1		In bed. ADOS & S.M.T.O. called	
	2		Div^n moving to St Louis. I left but did not move dump yet	
ST LOUIS	3.		Went to Dump in morning & searched for suitable spot near St Louis in afternoon. Decided on farm occupied by 26th Bty RGA who are moving tomorrow. Saw S.C. RA. as to gun & [illegible] of C/187, which latter Bty has treated with characteristic abandon	
	4.		Lorries from T'Hooghe arrived but RGA orders had been changed. After long delay pitched marquee & got office in a wretched scullery room with Belgians (refugees etc) always in & out.	
	5.		RTO sent truck containing clothing SD back unopened yesterday. Went to Bissegem accordingly to see him & wired Base for the stores	
VICHTE	7		Moved to Vichte poor accommodation, everything congested with Brit & French troops. Of course four of stores arrived as we were moving	
	9		Complained to DHQ as to units, Tp 125th Bty not drawing. Went to Corps, but ADOS out	
	10		DHQ moved to Caster. Went there in morning. ARMISTICE from 1100 hours 11 Nov	
NIEUWERBRAKEL	14.		Moved to Nieuwerbrakel. Have sent demands for 2nd blanket to Base & large demands for spit & polish clothing as Div^n moves to II from XIX Corps on being included in Div^ns to occupy Germany	Convoy
	15		Went to Corps at Courtrai & saw ADOS. Gas Respirator reserve sent to Base	
	16.		Units busy drawing & discarding stores which are not to be taken on march.	
	17.		Blankets arrived & a lot of vehicles. Railhead at Vichte - 25 miles off on a dreadful road - makes things more than difficult, especially when we shall be constantly moving forward & further from our railway line of supply	
SANTBERGEN	18		Moved to Santbergen. Heavy demands for clothing on G orders to get units spic & span	
	19.		QMG wired that clothing was only to be issued to replace unserviceable. This makes my position difficult as units have demanded heavily & I do not know what is indispensable & what merely ornamental. Stopped stores for next pack.	

2449 Wt. W14957/M90 750,000 1/16 J.B.C. & A. Forms/C.2118/12.

17

Instructions regarding War Diaries and Intelligence Summaries are contained in F. S. Regs., Part II. and the Staff Manual respectively. Title Pages will be prepared in manuscript.

WAR DIARY
or
~~INTELLIGENCE SUMMARY~~
(Erase heading not required.)

Army Form C. 2118.

DADOS 41 D

November 1918 (Sheet 2)

WO 31

Place	Date	Hour	Summary of Events and Information	Remarks and references to Appendices
GRAMMONT	Nov 21		Moved here. Got a good store at Goods Railway Siding.	
	23		Railhead changed to HERSEAUX nr. ROUBAIX. Went to 122 Bde HQ. Blankets arrived & spec. demands issued for horse shoes, just in time to borrow from 41st RA to enable 11 AOA Bde which has been starved in this rather store to tide over the time till next bulk consignment arrives	
	27		Railhead changed to TOURNAI	
	28		Div^n is now in X Corps & will come in a few days under Fourth Army	
	29		ADOS X Corps came. Large amount of horse shoes came up which relieves the situation as the 11th AOA Bde has been starved for stores to date. Will be able to carry on	

J. C. Sprague (?) Major
DADOS 41 Div^n

30/11/18

2449 Wt. W14957/M90 750,000 1/16 J.B.C. & A. Forms/C.2118/12.

Army Form C. 2118.

Instructions regarding War Diaries and Intelligence Summaries are contained in F. S. Regs., Part II. and the Staff Manual respectively. Title Pages will be prepared in manuscript.

DADOS. 41 Div.

WAR DIARY
or
INTELLIGENCE SUMMARY
(Erase heading not required.)

December 1918 (Sheet 1)

Vol 32

Place	Date	Hour	Summary of Events and Information	Remarks and references to Appendices
	December 1918			
GRAMMONT	2		Large quantity of clothing received from CALAIS – we are now to be based on HAVRE – on cancelled indent, which will cause a glut. Went to 123 Bde HQ	
	3		Have stopped stores loaded from yesterday. Heard this evening that Base was again changed to CALAIS. This constant condition of mutability makes it impossible to know what to do as of course bulk days are very different at the 2 Bases	
	4		Went to X Corps, & saw acting ADOS. also DADOS 34 Div. Wired HAVRE (on whom we are based till 6th as it now appears) for soap &c.	
	5		1 OMs now 26 (Med) BOSSONT 20 (light) FRESNOY. 47 (light) AVESNES. Railhead at GHISLENGHEIM today. Stores arrived today	
	6		Went to to Resident & 138 3rd Ambce. Div. move forward postponed to 12th Dec 8d.	
	8		Wire (2 days late) from CALAIS moving bulk from Schedule A, to which we had been previously shifted, to the original Schedule B. This merely makes confusion & delay worse confounded than ever	
	10		Have wired for horse shoes & grinding for issue on the march.	
	11		Div. starts to move to NAMUR area. We shall halt 2 days at BRAINE L'ALLEUD, to which I am sending on lorries. Railhead changes to BRAINE LE COMTE, to-morrow also. Excess clothing is being authorised in large quantities, which leaves the "ration" scale into high today. In my opinion troops do not seem to be badly clothed as a whole	
	12 to 14		Left GRAMMONT first stage to BRAINE L'ALLEUD, & proceeded by daily stages to KYSGHEM, HAL, BRAINE L'ALLEUD	
BRAINE L'ALLEUD	17		No stores came up before being moved to new railhead at GEMBLOUX. I went by stage via MORBOIS, MARY, WAVRE LA CHAUSSEE to VINALMONT	VINALMONT
	19		Went to 10 Army & saw DDOS.	
VINALMONT	20		Opened here to day. Railhead is HUY	
	21.		Went to HQ 123 Inf Bde. HQ Train & saw Area Cdt. HUY with a view to getting a store there	
	22.		1000 Lifebuoy blankets arrived. Went to 124 Inf Bde. & to DA.	
	23.		Started Dump at HUY. Blankets (2nd) began to arrive. Office remains at VINALMONT. Boot question, top repairs, is now acute	
	24.		Still no grinding. Went to Huy in morning	
	25.		Merry Xmas Dinner at HUY. No stores to-day	

2449 Wt. W14957/M90 750,000 1/16 J.B.C. & A. Forms/C.2118/12.

Instructions regarding War Diaries and Intelligence Summaries are contained in F. S. Regs., Part II. and the Staff Manual respectively. Title Pages will be prepared in manuscript.

DADOS 41 Divn.

WAR DIARY or ~~INTELLIGENCE SUMMARY~~

(Erase heading not required.)

December 1918 (Sheet 2)

Army Form C. 2118.

Place	Date	Hour	Summary of Events and Information	Remarks and references to Appendices
	December			
VIRALMONT	26		Stores arrived to day but no soap & still no grinding. however other kinds are arrived of "general stores" which ought to include it. Trucks take about 5 days from day of despatch to reach here. Went to HQrs re money [illegible]	
	28		Capt. BAILEY arrived for attachment. Q got particulars as to boots & grinding - for which there is of course a crying necessity - so as to urge Corps in view of probable early move. Nothing arrived to day	
	29		Still no stores. 124 Bde report that their units cannot move without 25 o/o of [illegible] boots.	
	30		Went to HQrs & HQ 122 Bde	
	31		Went to Fourth Army HQ., saw DDOS as to boots indent etc. Grinding & boots came to day but hopelessly insufficient under present circumstances and also belated.	
			31/12/1918	
			C Spencer Major DADOS 41 Div	

2449 Wt. W14957/M90 750,000 1/16 J.B.C. & A. Forms/C.2118/12.

Army Form C. 2118.

Instructions regarding War Diaries and Intelligence Summaries are contained in F. S. Regs., Part II. and the Staff Manual respectively. Title Pages will be prepared in manuscript.

DADOS.
41 Div.

WAR DIARY
or
~~INTELLIGENCE SUMMARY~~
(Erase heading not required.)

JANUARY 1919 (Sheet 1)

Place	Date	Hour	Summary of Events and Information	Remarks and references to Appendices
VINALMONT	JAN. 1919	1	Went to Huy, 124 Inf Bde & 26 R.F. Fetched a lot of German Clothes for distribution	
		2	Went to 123 Inf Bde	
		3.	Received orders to report to V. Corps, [illegible]. Capt. WATKINS appointed to succeed me	
		4	Went to Namur & saw DDOS. No boots yet	
		5	Truck of clothing rec'd but only contained 40 pairs Boots size 9 small quantity Sundry	
		6	Lt Col Spranger CBE left for V Corps. 41st Divn commenced entraining for Germany. No trucks in today	
		7	Major Watkins M.C arrived for duty. Saw R.T.O re moving trucks of store arriving after 10th.	
		8	Saw DAQMG re Area Stores arranging re move to Germany	
		9	Arranging re move to Germany - stores closed at Huy	
		10.	Commenced move, 4 lorries & 2 trucks stores, with personnel left during day.	
		11.	Arrived Coln.	
		12	(Sunday) Went to D.H.Q. & arranged quarters etc.	
WAHN.		13.	Went to Wahn, lorries unloaded - Officers returns cleared out & occupied.	
		14.	Went to Wahn - arranged with ADMS & O/C 139 F.A. for Ambulance Cars going to collect sick, should take stores for units in the neighbourhood.	
		15	Do. 20 Tons Stores arrived, good supply of boots & sundry, relieving the situation.	
		16.	Went to Wahn with D.A.Q.M.G. Railhead nearly cleared. Unable to [illegible] a car, so cannot visit units in outlying districts. DAQMG has promised to get me one, if at all possible.	

Army Form C. 2118.

Instructions regarding War Diaries and Intelligence Summaries are contained in F. S. Regs., Part II. and the Staff Manual respectively. Title Pages will be prepared in manuscript.

WAR DIARY
or
INTELLIGENCE SUMMARY
(Erase heading not required.)

Sheet 2

Place	Date	Hour	Summary of Events and Information	Remarks and references to Appendices
WAHN	17.		Saw O/c P of W. camp WAHN. found he did not require clothing which Cav. Corps had instructed me to demand, so cancelled Indent on Base. Pending authority from Army, O/c P of W camp is handing over part of his surplus of footsocks. 126 Army Bde R.F.A. joined 41st Div. from 4th Cav. Div.	
"	18.		Routine work at Wahn	
"	19		(Sunday) office work in morning.	
"	20		Visited 122 Bde. 15th Hants. 18th KRR. 26 R.F. & 19th Middsex. no complaints.	
"	21		Routine work. No car available.	
"	22		3 four lorries borrowed by Q. for E.F.C. for trip to Bonn Station. Full lorry load sent to 124 Bde.	
"	23.		Horseshoes & picketing gear arrived from Base. Stores sent to 122 Bde. Letter from W.O. ordering Capt Fanning's immediate release.	
"	24.		Very little doing, stores clear. Lorries to Railhead with Salvage.	
"	25.		Routine work.	
	26		(Sunday) office in morning - Hunting for new store, billets etc at DEUTZ with D.A.Q.M.G. Visited 124 Brigade. 1 Truck oil, soap - picketing gear etc arrived.	

2449 Wt. W14957/M90 750,000 1/16 J.B.C. & A. Forms/C.2118/12.

Army Form C. 2118.

Instructions regarding War Diaries and Intelligence Summaries are contained in F. S. Regs., Part II. and the Staff Manual respectively. Title Pages will be prepared in manuscript.

WAR DIARY
or
INTELLIGENCE SUMMARY
(Erase heading not required.)

Sheet 3.

Place	Date	Hour	Summary of Events and Information	Remarks and references to Appendices
	1919.			
WAHN.	27	Jan	Located new store, but unable to find suitable billets for men. Turned down those offered by civil authorities, totally unsuitable being half the ground floor of an 'out of bounds' Estaminet.	
"	28	"	Office – Rang up A.D.O.S. X Corps re demobilisation of Armourers attached to Infantry Bns: This to be done by D.D.O.S. & not by the Dn. Located office & billets – inspected them.	
"	29	"	Started moving office & stores from WAHN to DEUTZ. 13 LUISEN Str. for office. Store at 44 MATHILDEN Str. Salvage dump at HEUMAR. rail head.	
DEUTZ	30	"	Completed move. Visit from A.D.O.S. getting stores & office straight & in working order.	
"	31	"	Routine work. Obtained list of surplus stores from O/c R.P.O.W. camp WAHN. ~~to~~ handed over to [illegible] by Canadians. reported this. D.A.D.O.S.	
"	~~1~~	~~Feb.~~	~~Gen: routine work. 3 lorries urgently wanted by 'Q' to send 120 Bde. who are moving in.~~	
"	~~2~~	~~"~~	~~(Sunday)~~	
"	~~3~~	"	~~office. Visited Railhead HEUMAR. quite clear. 2 trucks salvage ([illegible]) [illegible] obtained [illegible].~~	

2449 Wt. W14957/M90 750,000 1/16 J.B.C. & A. Forms/C.2118/12.

Army Form C. 2118.

Instructions regarding War Diaries and Intelligence Summaries are contained in F. S. Regs., Part II. and the Staff Manual respectively. Title Pages will be prepared in manuscript.

DADOS 41st Div.

WAR DIARY
or
~~INTELLIGENCE SUMMARY~~

(Erase heading not required.)

Feb: 1919 Sheet 1.

Vol 34

Place	Date	Hour	Summary of Events and Information	Remarks and references to Appendices
DEUTZ.	1st Feb. 1919		No stores from Base. Sent 3 lorries to 'Q' for 123 Bde - who are moving -	
	2		(Sunday) Office routine in morning. 10 tons stores advised from Base. (1 truck)	
	3		Went to WAEUMAR visited salvage dump - 2 trucks salvage sent base yesterday. Went to 140th F.A. also to A.H.Q. re stores at R.P.O.W. camp.	
	4		Closed Div: Armourers shop, & returned 3 armourers to Infty Bns.	
	5		Office, visited 124 Bde Hoffungstall. all satisfied, also 122 & 123 Bdes. Wired A.H.Q. O, my requirements for Clothing etc. nil.	
	6		10 tons general stores received at railhead.	
	7		Saw A/Q 10th Queens re horseshoes. Routine work.	
	8		Routine	
	9		(Sunday). 3 Tons genl. stores received railhead.	
	10		Reply from R.P.O.W. that towels no longer required, Cancelled indent for 15.000. Stores sent to 124 Bde. 5 units.	
	11		Wired base hastening supplies horseshoes & soap & paint - all very short, & badly needed.	
	12		Truck with 8 Tons general stores arrived. Stores sent Arty. Bdes. Pte Keats sent for Tempy duty to O.O. II Army Troops, No 1.	
	13		Routine work	

2449 Wt. W14957/M90 750,000 1/16 J.B.C. & A. Forms/C.2118/12.

Army Form C. 2118.

Instructions regarding War Diaries and Intelligence Summaries are contained in F. S. Regs., Part II. and the Staff Manual respectively. Title Pages will be prepared in manuscript.

WAR DIARY or ~~INTELLIGENCE SUMMARY~~

(Erase heading not required.)

DADOS 41st Div — Feb. 1919 — 2nd Sheet.

Place	Date	Hour	Summary of Events and Information	Remarks and references to Appendices
DEUTZ	14		Went to Bonn to see A.D.O.S. re several matters – brought back 100 Flags u.s.	
"	15		Routine work.	
"	16	(Sunday)	Two trucks arrived with 79 Bales Clothing + 7 tons horseshoes + field stores. Spoke A.D.O.S. re site for I.C. station necessity for this Divn. He is referring to 2nd Army.	
"	17		My [illegible] Office work only. –	
"	18		Saw Army re stoppage of returned vehicles etc to Calais, Parking returned Ambulance vehicles at [illegible]	
"	19		8 Tons stores arrived. Put in requisition for 4000 Paillasses.	
"	20		Routine work. Paid the men. Sorting stores received yesterday.	
"	21		Issued stores to M.G. Corps. Arty Bde, 123 + 124 Bdes. Wire from A.D.O.S. instructing me to wire Calais to supply soft soap in lieu of yellow – explain situation to units, when offering them soft soap.	
"	22		Routine work. Stores sent out to 122 Bde. 4 Tons fuel stores advised.	
"	23	(Sunday)	8 Tons stores received at Railhead nearly all horseshoes. This relieves a serious situation.	

2449 Wt. W14957/M90 750,000 1/16 J.B.C. & A. Forms/C.2118/12.

Instructions regarding War Diaries and Intelligence Summaries are contained in F. S. Regs., Part II. and the Staff Manual respectively. Title Pages will be prepared in manuscript.

D.A.D.O.S. 41st Div.

WAR DIARY
or
INTELLIGENCE SUMMARY
(Erase heading not required.)

February 1919
3rd Sheet.

Army Form C. 2118.

Place	Date	Hour	Summary of Events and Information	Remarks and references to Appendices
DEUTZ	24.		6 Tons stores received at Railhead. Also 4 K.T. Boilers for 20th D.S.I.	
"	25		Routine.	
"	26		Capt Bailey left for Guards Division, as acting D.A.D.O.S. Saw Q.M. 10th Queens re their indents for Excess clothing & bicycles.	
"	27		4 Tons stores received, including Bath stores. Went to Bonn & collected 8 Rifles ·22. Saw B.G. 124 Bde. who is asking for a reserve of clothing. Got 2000 Paillasses from Guards Divn.	
"	28		Routine work.	
"	1 March		Went with D.A.Q.M.G. to 122, 123 & 124 Bdes. All satisfied with present position as to stores, except clothing. Apparently this neglect of Q.M.s to indent. Meeting of Q.M.s being called to go into this. Went to 2nd Army Troops Stores & got clothing etc. Large quantity horse rugs received of which I have no knowledge — no vouchers either.	
"	2	Sunday.		

2449 Wt. W14957/M90 750,000 1/16 J.B.C. & A. Forms/C.2118/12.

Army Form C. 2118.

Instructions regarding War Diaries and Intelligence Summaries are contained in F. S. Regs., Part II. and the Staff Manual respectively. Title Pages will be prepared in manuscript.

DADOS 41st Divn

WAR DIARY
or
~~INTELLIGENCE SUMMARY~~

(Erase heading not required.)

March 1919

Place	Date	Hour	Summary of Events and Information	Remarks and references to Appendices
Germany DEUTZ.	1 March		Went with DAQ [illegible] to 122. 123 & 124 Bdes. all satisfied with present position of supply of stores - except clothing. This is apparently due to neglect of QM's to indent, as none now outstanding. Meeting of QM's being called (123 Bde) to go into this. Called at 2nd A. Troops stores, & got clothing.	
	2	Sunday.	Office in morng. 8 Tons general stores arrived from base.	
	3		73 bales underclothing for baths arrived.	
	4		Got 20 bicycles from Guards Divn & 50 blankets, & saw N.Z. div. re their stores.	
	5		Routine work. 5 Tons genl. stores received from base.	
	6		Saw DADOS 34th div. re exchange of units bulk stores - routine.	
	7.		Sergt Duckwall arrived for tempy duty, from COO Cologne. Got stores from N.Z. Divn. Baths report German soap powder, no use at all - won't wash clothes. 1/2 ton was issued to them.	
	8		8 Tons genl stores from base. Sent 1000 paillasses to Bensberg for 23rd Middlesex Regt.	
	9.		(Sunday)	

2449 Wt. W14957/M90 750,000 1/16 J.B.C. & A. Forms/C.2118/12.

Instructions regarding War Diaries and Intelligence Summaries are contained in F. S. Regs., Part II. and the Staff Manual respectively. Title pages will be prepared in manuscript.

DADOS 41st Div

WAR DIARY
or
INTELLIGENCE SUMMARY.
(Erase heading not required.)

March 1919.

Army Form C. 2118.

Place	Date	Hour	Summary of Events and Information	Remarks and references to Appendices
DEUTZ	10	–	A.A.&Q.M.G. inspected Stores & office. Brought units of 122 Bde. with Stores. Good supply of Sundries up in last consignment. Issued 900 Paillasses to M.G. Bde.	
	11.		Meeting of Quartermasters at DADOS office. very good attendance. Shortage of Soap & brooms, chief causes of complaint. Everything else pretty good.	
	12		Went to NZ. div. drew Chaff cutters (6) etc. 9 Tons General Stores rec^d from base.	
	13.		Routine work.	
	14		Ditto – chiefly on demob. & barrack equipment returns.	
	15.		9 tons Genl Stores received from Base. also 79 cases box Respirators & containers for Divnl Reserves.	
	16		Sunday. Closed office in afternoon.	
	17		Routine work.	
	18		6 Tons Genl Stores received from Base. Big discrepancies of soap etc reported.	
	19		Saw A.A.&Q.M.G. re position of soap. This has been very short, but last bulk returns were issued almost in full. Went N.Z. div. re Trench Mortars & Equipment.	
	20.		Routine work	
	21		Attended Major Cunninghame's funeral as Pall bearer in morning. In afternoon office work – pay etc.	

Instructions regarding War Diaries and Intelligence Summaries are contained in F. S. Regs., Part II. and the Staff Manual respectively. Title pages will be prepared in manuscript.

D.A.D.O.S. London Divn

WAR DIARY or INTELLIGENCE SUMMARY.

(Erase heading not required.)

March 1919.

Army Form C. 2118.

Place	Date	Hour	Summary of Events and Information	Remarks and references to Appendices
DEUTZ	22.		Attached to VI Corps on 21st. Sent all returns necessary to A.D.O.S. VI Corps.	Collected 15 pistols webley from Bonn.
	23	(Sunday)	5 Tons general stores. mostly clothing received from Base.	
	24.		Routine work.	
	25		Meeting of Quartermasters Nr Mée. All units well off with stores. no complaints.	
	26		A.D.O.S. VI Corps called. 12 Tons general stores recd from base.	
	27		Routine work. A certain amount of duplication of stores, Base not cancelling indents as advised, & stores having been obtained from N.Z. divn. These will soon work off in satisfying future demands.	
	28.		Routine work. collecting stores from N.Z. dump.	
	29		Saw QM. 17th Fusiliers. who have just joined the Divn. New drafts to them arrived badly clothed.	
	30		(Sunday) 126 A.F.A. Bde. moving from London div: to II Corps.	
	31.		4 tons general stores recd from base.	

C. T. Walters Major
D.A.D.O.S. London Divn

T2134. Wt. W708—776. 500000. 4/15. Sir J. C. & S.

Instructions regarding War Diaries and Intelligence Summaries are contained in F. S. Regs., Part II. and the Staff Manual respectively. Title pages will be prepared in manuscript.

D.A.D.O.S. London Div.

WAR DIARY or INTELLIGENCE SUMMARY.

(Erase heading not required.)

April 1919.

Army Form C. 2118.

Place	Date	Hour	Summary of Events and Information	Remarks and references to Appendices
Cöln				
DEUTZ.	1	Apl.	Five tons genl. stores received.	
	2		Saw A.D.O.S. went into question of salvage with him. & system of checking receipts.	
	3		Collecting cooking appliances for large draft Y.S. now arriving from N.Z. div. arranged with ~~A.D.O.S.~~ for Capt Bailey to come here daily whilst I am on leave.	
	4		Major Walker M.C. proceeded on leave & Capt. Bailey M.C. took over	
	5		Routine work	
	6		Visited A.D.O.S. re reformation of T.M. Batteries. 4 Ton General Stores received	
	7		Inspected 12" Bad Survey Cadre Unit, unserviceable equipment & visited I.O.M. re inspection of vehicles which we carried out same day.	
	8		Routine work	
	9		Applied to C.O.O. Cologne for 600 Tubs washing, routine work etc. 4 Tons General Stores recd.	
	10		Conference of Q.M.S. everything satisfactory. 50 Store Sheds obtained on loan from C.O.O. Cologne for forward areas	
	11		Received 600 Tubs washing for forward areas. Inspected vehicle 19" Mdx at Linde 8 marquees obtained from New Zealand Unit for Sports.	
	12		Indent to complete T.M. Batteries cancelled by Calais & A.D.O.S.. visited A.D.O.S. with reference to this. have written him for instructions. Visited I.O.M. for condemnation certificate for vehicle for 19" Mdx.	

T2134. Wt. W708—776. 500000. 4/15. Sir J. C. & S.

WADOS
London Divn

Instructions regarding War Diaries and Intelligence Summaries are contained in F. S. Regs., Part II. and the Staff Manual respectively. Title pages will be prepared in manuscript.

WAR DIARY
or
INTELLIGENCE SUMMARY.
(Erase heading not required.)

April 1919

Army Form C. 2118.

Place	Date	Hour	Summary of Events and Information	Remarks and references to Appendices
Cöln Deuty	Apl	13	1000 Paillasses del^d to 122 Brigade. 21 Stoves Soyers on loan to Right & Left Brigade forward area. 18000 rds Dummy Ammn demanded. Tubs washing dist^n to Hvy Brigade. Fly Sprayers muslin & Traps demanded from Base for Divn	
		14	8 Tons General Stores recd. ADOS VI Corps & Col. Fuller visited the Stores & office. Obtained 1 Anvil from New Zealand Unit for Animal Collecting Camp.	
		15	Saw DAQMG re requisitioning Stoves & Cap wire. 5 Tons General Stores received	
		16	Interviewed candidate of 2/4 Queen's for attachment to RAOC. TMB Office 122 Brigade visited re Stores. OC Sanitary Section called re Buckets Latrine. Stores issued to all Brigades today	
		17	Visited Q re Tents CSL for 2nd London Brigade. Saw DOS re Demobilisation mob Tables & Indents. Routine work. OC Divl Train called re Paint & Brushes for Transport wagons & vehicles.	
		18	COO Cologne unable to issue Tents CSL till 22nd. Saw DAQG, arranged to issue 6 Marquees operating to 2nd London Brigade temporarily, wired Calais for 60 Flags red for range purposes	
		19	Visited DADOS re Web equipment, asked Q to issue DRO calling for indents, visited COO Cologne re Tents. 2nd London Brigade moved to Gepelskirchen. Routine work	
		20	25 Tents drawn & issued to 26 RF for isolation camp. routine work.	
		21	ADOS visited office re demobilisation. Visited COO Cologne re Tents. Arranged with "Q" for 12 Lorries & 48 men to report at office 7.45 am 22nd.	

T2134. Wt. W708—776. 500000. 4/15. Sir J. C. & S.

D.A.D.O.S.
London Division

Instructions regarding War Diaries and Intelligence Summaries are contained in F. S. Regs., Part II. and the Staff Manual respectively. Title pages will be prepared in manuscript.

WAR DIARY
or
INTELLIGENCE SUMMARY.
(Erase heading not required.)

April 1919

Army Form C. 2118.

Place	Date	Hour	Summary of Events and Information	Remarks and references to Appendices
Cologne	Apl	22	Meeting of Q.M.s. Drew 450 Tents from C.O.O. Cologne. Issued 80 to O.O. Corps Troops. Visited A.D.O.S. re Unit Register Cards. Visited Army re Tent Bottoms and arranged for Captain Bailey to remain with London Division until Major Watkins returns from leave	
Duty		23.	600 Latrine Buckets issued, visited A.D.O.S. re blanket return & issue to bring up to 3 for each man. Wrote C.O.O. Cologne re issue of 50 Stoves Soyer on loan for race meeting. Visited [illegible] to condemn Wagon G.S. unserviceable, visited Railhead & Salvage Dump.	
		24	Wrote C.O.O. Cologne re issuing paint for Div. Train to be replaced by paint due from Base. Routine work. Issued 20 pails [illegible] to Q.M. Race meeting on loan also 4 marquees [illegible] & 12 Tents [illegible] all on loan.	L
		25	Visited 1st & 2nd London Brigades only queries relating to Ground Sheets & webbing equipment both of which have been dealt with. Visited Railhead & Dump. Letter from C.O.O. Cologne regretting cannot issue Stoves Soyer owing to heavy demands having used up his stock.	
		26	Visited New Zealand unit re Stoves Soyer etc for Race meeting. Visited C.O.O. Cologne & O.C. [illegible] re tents washing. Col. Shine gave verbal authority to requisition, Routine work.	
		27	Routine work	
		28	Major A.T. Watkins M.C. returned from leave and Captain Bailey [illegible] proceeded to D.O.S. office. Routine work. Made arrangements for moving Stores and Office to School buildings near Suspension bridge. 9 tons [illegible] Stores received	
		29.	A.I.A. (Lt Latham) called, requesting that all Lewis, Hotchkiss & AA guns including spare parts in the Division be overhauled weekly by Armourers. Routine work. (Divisional Races).	
		30.	Packing up office etc. Moved into School buildings – stores also moving – all now under one roof.	

D. D. & L., London, E.C.
(A8004) Wt. W1771/M2 31 750,000 5/17 Sch. 52 Forms/C2118/14

D.A.D.O.S. London Division.

Instructions regarding War Diaries and Intelligence Summaries are contained in F. S. Regs., Part II. and the Staff Manual respectively. Title pages will be prepared in manuscript.

WAR DIARY
or
~~INTELLIGENCE SUMMARY.~~
(Erase heading not required.)

May 1919

Army Form C. 2118.

Place	Date	Hour	Summary of Events and Information	Remarks and references to Appendices
DEUTZ.	MAY 1		General holiday for Germans. no trams etc. Unable to procure car. 2 lorries delivering stores to 122 & 123 Bdes. Went 'Q' office re tents for 17th RF Bn. going out from Bensberg Bks. under canvas.	
	2.		Went to 'Q' office re demands for excess & unauthorised stores. A.D.O.S. called, went into several questions with him. Visited Railhead & Salvage dump at Heumar.	
	3.		Visit from DAQMG who inspected stores etc. 6 tons general stores received from base. Visited 'Q' office re tents for 17th RF. Closed stores for 1/2 day	
	4		Sunday. office in morning. very quiet. Sorting stores received yesterday.	
	5.–		Routine work.	
	6.		8 tons General Stores received. Meeting of Quartermasters: tables & forms urgently required by those under canvas. Visited Army & received instructions re these & beds. went to VI Corps HQrs. A.D.O.S. on leave. a/A.D.O.S. out.	
	7.		a/A.D.O.S. visited stores. went into several matters with him re tents etc. Stores sent to 3rd Infty Bde. Lorry to Depot to collect 64 Tent bottoms. Visited O.M. M. Gun Bn. re their indent for tables etc.	
	8		Tent bottoms sent to 3rd Infty Bde. Collecting 100 Tents from Cologne depot for 3rd Bde. Arranged for 4 lorries to deliver these. Saw Camp Commandant re his indents.	

D. D. & L. London, E.C. (A8001) Wt. W1771/M2031 750,000 5/17 Sch. 52 Forms C2118/14

Instructions regarding War Diaries and Intelligence Summaries are contained in F. S. Regs., Part II. and the Staff Manual respectively. Title pages will be prepared in manuscript.

D A D O S
London Div.

WAR DIARY
or
~~INTELLIGENCE SUMMARY.~~
(Erase heading not required.)

May 1919.
2nd Sheet.

Army Form C. 2118.

Place	Date	Hour	Summary of Events and Information	Remarks and references to Appendices
DEUTZ.	9th May		Visited "Q" Office. re tents etc. AA & QMG visited Office & dump. Saw Staff Capt 2nd Bde. re their returns as to tent requirements.	
	10.		Visited 3rd Bde HQ qtrs & 17th RF's. 9 Tons general stores received from base.	
	11		Sunday	
	12.		~~Sunday~~ Visited German salvage dump. went to Volberg 9th E. Surreys etc. Drew 3 telescopic rifles from O.O. Rhine Troops.	
	13		Drawing Tent bottoms & Tents from Depot for 17th RF's. saw O/c 187 Bde RFA re their indents for Directors etc.	
	14		10 Tons genl stores arrived from base. Handed £109 & ~~[illegible]~~ Medals to O/c Cadre Bn. 12 East Surreys. leaving on 21st inst.	
	15		Delivered stores to 3rd L.Infy Bde. arranged with CRE. re issue of wood & nails in lieu of Tables & Forms.	
	16.		Truck no 87150 arrived from Base. issued stores to 1st & 2nd Bde. Payday.	
	17		Visited Q. — Saw Q.M. 23rd Middlesex & O.M. D.A. re their repainting helmets. Losses of clothing in last truck reported R.O.O. Pilfering is far too constant — Needed Army Ord. to exchange of Winter Clothing etc. —	

(A8001) Wt. W1771/M2031 750,000 5/17 D. D. & L., London, E.C. Sch. 52 Forms C2118/14

D. A. D. O. S. London Divn

Instructions regarding War Diaries and Intelligence Summaries are contained in F. S. Regs., Part II. and the Staff Manual respectively. Title pages will be prepared in manuscript.

WAR DIARY
or
INTELLIGENCE SUMMARY.
(Erase heading not required.)

May 1919

Army Form C. 2118.

Place	Date	Hour	Summary of Events and Information	Remarks and references to Appendices
DEUTZ	18th	–	Sunday. ½ day only. Delivered stores to 3rd Bde. clothing etc.	
	19.	–	Collected 330 Tents from Base depot Nippes & delivered 100 to 7/4 Queens bal. to 17th R.F. 41st Bn M.G.C. & No 4 Coy Div Train.	
	20.	–	Visited 1st Bde HdQrs. – salvage dump at Heumar – & 23rd Middsx at Bensberg Schloss. Officers meeting. 6 tons general stores received from base.	
	21.		Routine work. Sgt Bolton went sick with 'flu.	
	22.		All lorries delivering stores. Instructions to draw 100 Tents from 42 M.G. Bn & 10 Marquees also about 30 Tents from [illegible] Platz & to store these pending instructions from Q.	
	23.		Collecting tents from M.G. Bn. etc. 3 S/Sgt Armourers reported for duty, to relieve releasable armourers in Bns. Detailed S/Sgt Bullen to 19th Middsx. – S/Sgt Cooper to 11th Queens. to relieve S/Sgt Kirkby, & Arm Sgt Haynes to M.G. Bn to relieve S/Sgt Day. Advised by 'Q' that G.O.C. has ordered 3rd blanket to be withdrawn, & stored under Divnl arrangements, until Corps authority obtained. 'Phoned ADOS re this.	
	24.		The Marquees collected from M.G. Bn in very bad condition, folded up when wet & several completely spoilt. Reported to Q. Delivered stores to 2nd Inf Bde. Obtained 2 more large rooms for storing paillasses etc.	
	25.		Sunday. Divisional officers trip up the Rhine. – Weak.	

D. D. & L., London, E.C. (A8001) Wt. W1771/M2031 750,000 5/17 Sch. 52 Forms C2118/14

Instructions regarding War Diaries and Intelligence Summaries are contained in F. S. Regs., Part II. and the Staff Manual respectively. Title pages will be prepared in manuscript.

D.A.D.O.S. London Div:

WAR DIARY or INTELLIGENCE SUMMARY.

(Erase heading not required.)

May 1919.

Army Form C. 2118.

Place	Date	Hour	Summary of Events and Information	Remarks and references to Appendices
DEUTZ	26.		Delivered stores to 3rd Ldn. Bde. saw Q.M. 1/7th Middlx. Sent machine gun return to A.D.O.S. & queried shortages with Infty Bde & R.F.A. Procured 2 fresh wagons for stowage of paillasses & beds. now arriving. A.D.O.S. called re personnel for Corps I.C.S. 9 Tons Genl. stores received from Base. & 1 Cart water tank for D.A.C. Div's	
	27.		19th Mdsx. & 9th East Surreys came in re indents. Blankets etc. Phoned A.D.O.S. I could give him one W.O. for his I.C.S. but could not spare any storemen. 11 Tons genl stores recd. The Salvage dump at Heuman being very busy with returned boots etc. Detailed for	
	28.	-	visit from G.O.C. London Div: who appeared quite satisfied with everything. 10.00 hrs. There all day. 9 tons Board of Enquiry on a Fire at Arty Depôt Nippes. Genl stores received from base.	
	29.		At Nippes after 11 o'c. Office until then, & after lunch. S/Cdr Parker to go	
	30.		Routine work. A.D.O.S. visited me re sending 1 W.O. to Corps I.C.S. on return from leave. 10 men from R.F.A. arrived for duty with R.A.O.C.	
	31.		15 Tons Genl. stores recd from Base. Beds & paillasses arriving in large quantities. Saw O.O. Base Depot Cologne re summer clothing - on Enquiry board at Nippes until 2 o/c. 3 men for attachment to R.A.O.C. examined & records passed to A.D.O.S.	

D. D. & L., London, E.C. (A8001) Wt. W1771/M2031 750,000 5/17 Sch. 52 Forms C2118/14

Instructions regarding War Diaries and Intelligence Summaries are contained in F. S. Regs., Part II. and the Staff Manual respectively. Title pages will be prepared in manuscript.

D.A.D.O.S. London Division

WAR DIARY
or
~~INTELLIGENCE~~ SUMMARY.
(Erase heading not required.)

June 1919. Sheet 1.

Army Form C. 2118.

Place	Date	Hour	Summary of Events and Information	Remarks and references to Appendices
DEV+Z.	June 1.		Sunday. Office work in morning.	
	2.		At Zippe's all morning on Inf Board. Visited C.O.O. Cologne Depot re sun curtains etc. These will not be issued. Delivered stores to 3rd Lond. Bde.	
	3.		12 Tons general stores received from base. Delivering to 3rd Bde. Arranged for Bdes to collect summer clothing tomorrow from Ordnance Base depot. Detailed 2 of my lorries to assist. Saw Q.M. 23rd Mdsex Regt. King's birthday. Office closed at 12. am	
	4.		Meeting of Inf enquiry board at Cologne. Office in aftn.	
	5.		Visited 9th East Surreys. met Staff Capt 1 Bde. & QM's of 1/7 Middlesex + 23rd Mdsex there re their outstanding indent. Found items outstanding for the whole Bde practically nil. Great slackness is evident in units not demanding stores from their Q.M.'s + when inspected by G.O.C's stating that stores are either on indent or unobtainable from Ordnance. Have had a good deal of trouble re this lately, but was able to satisfy the Divisional G.O.C. that the Division was very well looked after by Ordnance.	
	6.		Office work - indents etc. Saw CRE re beds, ladders etc. + 228 Field Coy re Lewis guns. Wired demand for 10 Lewis guns to Corps for approval to complete Field Coys RE to establishment.	

D. D. & L., London, E.C.
(A8001) Wt. W1771/M2031 750,000 5/17 Sch. 52 Forms/C2118/14

Instructions regarding War Diaries and Intelligence Summaries are contained in F. S. Regs., Part II. and the Staff Manual respectively. Title pages will be prepared in manuscript.

~~DADOS~~ London Div.

WAR DIARY
or
INTELLIGENCE SUMMARY.
(Erase heading not required.)

June 1919.

(2)

Army Form C. 2118.

Place	Date	Hour	Summary of Events and Information	Remarks and references to Appendices
Deutz.	7.	June	Sent wests to 1st London Inf Bde. No car available for many days to unable to visit units. Routine paper work.	
	8.		Sunday. 2 trucks with 459 sacks web equipment received from base Lorries clearing railhead.	
	9.		Whit Monday. Office closed early. 4 Tons general stores received from Base.	
	10.		Attended meeting of Court of Enquiry re fire at Nippes. 10 Tons general stores received from Base. Passed a file of indents & requisitions ~~for~~ demands by Units under Cavalry 7+ circular for revision to Div. Q. Units demanding many unnecessary things.	Dgls.
	11.		Visited A.D.O.S. re personnel question. Offl Furniture Dgls to ADOS office. Ptes Patterson, Colbert & Annger left for England on demobilisation.	
	12.		Arranged fatigue party from 9th E. Surreys to sort web Equipment. Paper work increasing fast in office, leave little time for anything else.	
	13.		Routine work.	
	14.		Visited Q. and Cologne depôt re drawing Pimlico & Lee 9 stores. 12 tons genl stores received from Base.	
	15.		Sunday. —	

D. D. & L., London, E.C.
(A8001) Wt. W1771/M2031 750,000 5/17 Sch. 52 Forms C2118/14

Instructions regarding War Diaries and Intelligence Summaries are contained in F. S. Regs., Part II. and the Staff Manual respectively. Title pages will be prepared in manuscript.

DADOS London Div

WAR DIARY ~~or INTELLIGENCE SUMMARY.~~

(Erase heading not required.)

June 1919

(3)

Army Form C. 2118.

Place	Date	Hour	Summary of Events and Information	Remarks and references to Appendices
DEUTZ	16.	June	Office work. No cars as usual. Delivering stores to 3rd Lond Bde. Fatigue party from 9th E. Surreys sorting web equipment	
	17	"	Orders received re 'J' day. 10 tons genl. stores received from Base. Quartermasters meeting. No complaints. Wired for A/S/Sgt Faulkner to report to me, to take charge of lorry for M.G. spares. These to be drawn tomorrow.	
	18	"	A/S/Sgt Faulkner arrived from 17th R.F. Vickers guns & spares received from O.O. VI Corps Troops. Visit by DADOS "Light" Div re his move. delivered stores to 3rd Bde. Arranging details of move.	
	19		Drew 16 Magazines from OO Nippes & sent them out to 3rd Bde Overath. Drew balance of M.G.'s and spare parts to complete lorry of these stores. In afternoon drew 100 C&L tents, & sent 80 to 3rd Bde 20 to 2nd Bde.	
	20.	"	Visited Army, re drawing 16 Lewis guns for Div training - as these must be handed in to ICS for GHQ pool, agreed not to draw until present position cleared up. Cancelled outstanding indents for School of Gunnery - now disbanded.	
	21.		Attended conference at GHQ. re proposals as to method of demanding stores from base, in view of reduced personnel at base etc. Calais suggest that all detail stores should be bulked in future. With the present depleted staff this will entail more work for DADOS than can be managed as expeditiously & accurately as hitherto. D.O.S. is trying to avoid this.	

D. D. & L., London, E.C. (A8001) Wt. W1771/M2031 750,000 5/17 Sch. 52 Forms C2118/14

Instructions regarding War Diaries and Intelligence Summaries are contained in F. S. Regs., Part II, and the Staff Manual respectively. Title pages will be prepared in manuscript.

D.A.D.O.S. London Div

WAR DIARY or INTELLIGENCE SUMMARY.

(Erase heading not required.)

June 1919 (4)

Army Form C. 2118.

Place	Date	Hour	Summary of Events and Information	Remarks and references to Appendices
Deutz.	22		Sunday, Visited all Field Ambulances and many other units. Englesknchen. Lindlar etc. 6 Tons general stores received from Base.	
	23.		12 Tons general stores rec^d from Base & balance of Web Equipment. Dump ~~Store~~ very congested with stores, as delivery to units is being delayed, until the situation is settled. L/Cpl Le Page proceed for demobilisation	
	24.		Advised that the Hun has promised to sign Peace treaty. Sorting out stores & delivering to all units that can accept.	
	25.		Returns & indents & interviewing O.R's all the morning. Cadre equip^t of 138 F.A. reported ready for inspection, arranged with D.A.D.M.S. to inspect this tomorrow.	
	26.		Visited Urbach and inspected equipment of 138 Field Amb. Cadre. Very good condition, & very trifling amount of lotes U. Arranged with 'G' for a guard on D.A.D.O.S. dump. A/Cpl Stacey went on leave to U.K.	
	27.		Routine work.	
	28.		Do. Peace signed.	
	29.		Sunday.	
	30.		S/Cdr White left for demobilisation. Cpl Lelding (Office) left for leave to U.K.	

DADOS London Div.

Instructions regarding War Diaries and Intelligence Summaries are contained in F. S. Regs., Part II. and the Staff Manual respectively. Title pages will be prepared in manuscript.

WAR DIARY
or
~~INTELLIGENCE SUMMARY.~~

(Erase heading not required.)

July 1919

Army Form C. 2118.

Place	Date	Hour	Summary of Events and Information	Remarks and references to Appendices
DEUTZ.	1.		Routine work.	
	2		attended conference of AA & QMG. staff captains & Bdes. Quartermasters etc at each of the 3 Brigades. Ovrath & Melfrest. Paint for steel helmets causing trouble as units unable to mix required colour.	
	3		General holiday for all troops. Closed the dump.	
	4		Drawing stores from Cologne base depôt. Truck arrived with about 12 tons stores from Calais base. Stores very congested owing to large quantity drawn from Cologne.	
	5.		Visited Railhead & Salvage dump. & No 2 Train A.S.C. Returned all the M.G. spares to C.O.O. supplies - which were drawn in anticipation of an advance of the Divn. Returned lorry to M.T. Cpl Keats returned to U.K. on death of Mother.	
	6		Sunday.	
	7.		Cologne base now functioning for all bulk stores. Indents & returns all day.	
	8		Visited D.O.S. Advised all units dates the indents due to reach me, also method of indenting. Put up indent for paint for steel helmets to Corps for authority. Stores nearly all cleared by & to units.	
	9.		Visit from ADOS. Signing indents etc all day. 316 beds delivered by German firm	

(A8001) D. D. & L., London, E.C. Wt. W1771/M2031 750,000 5/17 Sch. 52 Forms C2118/14

Instructions regarding War Diaries and Intelligence Summaries are contained in F. S. Regs., Part II. and the Staff Manual respectively. Title pages will be prepared in manuscript.

D.A.D.O.S.
London Division

WAR DIARY
or
~~INTELLIGENCE SUMMARY.~~
(Erase heading not required.)

July 1919.

Army Form C. 2118.

Place	Date	Hour	Summary of Events and Information	Remarks and references to Appendices
DEUTZ	10	–	Sending out beds etc. 800 sets tent boards to be drawn from C.O.S. Cologne. applied for 20 lorries and a fatigue party for tomorrow to collect & deliver, as per 'Q' distribution. 1st day Cologne races. As all the men have been working very hard & well of late, gave them half holiday.	
	11	–	Drawing tent boards, & delivering them. Saw QM. 9th East Surreys. Paper work all day.	
	12	–	Routine work: Lorries still delivering tent bottoms.	
	13	–	Sunday. Sent in Bulk indents to Cologne Base depot.	
	14	–	4 Tons General stores received from Base. Went to HQ re several questions.	
	15	–	Indents & correspondence all morning. Saw QM 23 Mdsx Regt all [illegible] in that Bn. Drew 4 Lewis guns from Nippes Depot, completing the 16 for Training purposes for the Divn.	
	16	–	Routine work.	
	17	–	Advice that bal of web Equipment is now available – drawing from Cologne. also 15 Lewis guns, for Field Coys R.E. Saw QM 7th E Surreys re their indents. Surplus bayonet fighting Equipment to be sent to Calais.	
	18		Depot will not issue Web Equipment until 25th arranged for 1 NCO & 6 men from 2nd Bde to come on that day to help sort it out. Drawing stores from Cologne (bulk)	
	19		General Peace holiday – stores closed all day.	

D. D. & L., London, E.C. (A5001) Wt. W1771/M2031 750,000 5/17 Sch. 52 Forms C2118/14

Instructions regarding War Diaries and Intelligence Summaries are contained in F. S. Regs., Part II. and the Staff Manual respectively. Title pages will be prepared in manuscript.

WAR DIARY or INTELLIGENCE SUMMARY.

(Erase heading not required.)

D.A.D.O.S. London Divn — July 1919

Army Form C. 2118.

Place	Date	Hour	Summary of Events and Information	Remarks and references to Appendices
Deutz	20.		Sunday. Returns etc. sorting stores drawn on Friday last	
	21.		10 tons stores arrived from Base. Drew tent poles for 2/4 Queens. Drew Medal Ribbon (British War Medal) for the Division.	
	22.		Routine work. 580 iron beds received.	
	23.		Routine work. drew 15 tents for 19th Middx.	
	24		Saw QM 2/4 Queens. Small instalment of stores arrived demanded under D of W. Cir 74	
	25.		Working on indents all morning. Drawing stores from Cologne Base depot. 15 tents & boards delivered to 19th Middx.	
	26		Indents, bulk indents, queries & correspondence all morning. Drawing tents & marquees from Cologne Depot. Instructed Q (Divn) re quoting Army Authority on demands for tentage.	
	27		Sunday Returns etc	
	28		Major C. T. Watkins MC proceeded on leave to UK. Major A. Needham MC assumed duties of a/DADOS.	

D. D. & L., London, E.C. (A8001) Wt. W1771/M2031 750,000 5/17 Sch. 52 Forms C2118/14

DADOS London Div

Instructions regarding War Diaries and Intelligence Summaries are contained in F. S. Regs., Part II. and the Staff Manual respectively. Title pages will be prepared in manuscript.

WAR DIARY
or
INTELLIGENCE SUMMARY.

(Erase heading not required.)

August 1919

Army Form C. 2118.

Place	Date	Hour	Summary of Events and Information	Remarks and references to Appendices
Deutz.	29.		Major C T Walters returned from leave from U.K. Major A V Needham handed over.	
	30		Routine work in morning. Cologne race meeting in afternoon.	
	31		Sunday. –	
	[illegible]		Routine Work.	

D. D. & L., London, E.C.
(A8001) Wt. W1771/M2031 750,000 5/17 Sch. 52 Forms/C2118/14

D.A.D.O.S. London Divn.

Instructions regarding War Diaries and Intelligence Summaries are contained in F. S. Regs., Part II. and the Staff Manual respectively. Title pages will be prepared in manuscript.

WAR DIARY
or
INTELLIGENCE SUMMARY.
(Erase heading not required.)

September 1919

Army Form C. 2118.

Place	Date	Hour	Summary of Events and Information	Remarks and references to Appendices
DEUTZ.	1.		Collected paint from R.E. Dump. Overalls. Gave the staff ½ day to go to Divisional sports, in which several taking part.	
	2		Visited Railhead & Salvage dump Heumar. Sgt Morgan sent to Heumar for tempy duty, taking stock. 3 R.F.A. men arrived for duty with R.A.O.C.	
	3.		Went to Bonn Tor Station, saw R.O.O. ref ~~[illegible]~~ destination U stores returned through him. Went to VI Corps to see A.D.O.S. ref. U stores. Took A.D.O.S. to Railhead Heumar, & Salvage dump. Corps order that all demands for Trucks required in future to be made to D.D.O.S. direct. Instructed salvage dump accordingly.	
	4.		Bdr Nuttall sent to Heumar to superintend the cleaning up, & proper storage of salvage returned. Cdr Davison sent G.H.Q. to consult O/c Personnel re pay of transferred R.F.A. men. Visit from A.D.O.S. re clearing U vehicles from Heumar railhead.	
	5.		Visited C.O.O. Base depot Nippes re return of salvage etc. Instructed to send all U stores to I.C.S. for conditioning & not direct to Depot. Arranged to draw 3 Travelling kitchens (bodies) for 2/4 Queens, today.	
	6		Cpl Geddes promoted to a/Sub Conductor. A.D.O.S. instructs me not to return salvage to VI Corps I.C.S. until he has confirmed C.O.O.'s instructions.	

D. D. & L., London, E.C. (A8004) Wt. W1771/M2 31 750,000 5/17 Sch. 52 Forms/C2118/14

DADOS London Div.

Instructions regarding War Diaries and Intelligence Summaries are contained in F. S. Regs., Part II. and the Staff Manual respectively. Title pages will be prepared in manuscript.

WAR DIARY
or
~~INTELLIGENCE SUMMARY.~~
(Erase heading not required.)

September 1919

Army Form C. 2118.

Place	Date	Hour	Summary of Events and Information	Remarks and references to Appendices
Deutz	7		Sunday.	
	8		Visited Hennar railhead & salvage dump. Railhead now cleared except 1 wagon Ambulance. Send 20 tent bottoms to R.F. (17th Bn) Spoke G.H.Q. D.O.S. re issue of Allied riband. They say no instructions received yet.	
	9		Routine work. Sent 17 marquees to Overath on loan for Div! horse show. S/Sgt Finch reported for duty, from DADOS Cavalry Corps.	
	10.		Routine work. Visited G.H.Q. re promotion of Pte Morgan to Actg Sergt. Put same for approval to A.D.O.S.	
	11		Routine work. Car not available. Wrote A.D.O.S. reference return of requisition stores. & also to try & move Aux. Horse Coy A.S.C. so that I can move my salvage dump from Hennar to Deutz.	
	12		Car not available. Drawing from Base depot. Sent 30 lamps F.S. to 2/4 Queens. Saw Q.M. 139 F.A. sent him to Whippies for spare parts of water cart.	
	13		Office work. returns etc.	
	14		Sunday.	
	15.		Drew 4 marquees from Depot for Div! Horseshow, Overath. Supplies of Indian Clothing & small size pantaloons not arriving – Reported this to A.D.O.S.	

D. D. & L., London, E.C.
(A8904) Wt. W1771/M2 3? 750000 5/17 Sch. 52 Forms/C2118/14

Instructions regarding War Diaries and Intelligence Summaries are contained in F. S. Regs., Part II. and the Staff Manual respectively. Title pages will be prepared in manuscript.

D.A.D.O.S. London Div.

Army Form C. 2118.

WAR DIARY
or
INTELLIGENCE SUMMARY.
(Erase heading not required.)

September 1919.

Place	Date	Hour	Summary of Events and Information	Remarks and references to Appendices
Deutz.	16		Divisional holiday. Horseshow. Store closed.	
	17		Major AO Needham relieved Major C.S. Walker who left on 3 days special leave to U.K.	
	18		Sent stores to 3rd London Bde.	
	19		Drawing stores from Cologne base	
	20	-	Routine work.	
	21	-	Sunday. - Major C.S. Walker returned from special leave.	
	22		Routine work. Divl Q. ask for 3rd blanket to be issued to Units under canvas. Spoke A.D.O.S. who instructs that this must be approved by Army Q.	
	23.		approval to draw 600 blankets phoned by Corps Q. arranged for six lorries to report tomorrow to draw these & deliver a part to M.G.C. Routine work.	
	24		Routine work. 6 lorries drawing & delivering blankets.	
	25.		Issued 100 beds on loan to Remount Camp. routine work.	
	26.		Drawing stores from Base depot. Saw 'Q' re supplies for Remount camp. 200 horses being sent in. - Routine work. Wrote A.D.O.S. re disposal of about 1000 beds, which are in my dump - surplus.	
	27.		Collected stores for new Animal reception camp. Humboldts factory, Rope, bag nose, also issued tables, forms, beds etc for 50 personnel. Routine work. -	
	28.		Sunday	

(A8004) Wt. W1771/M 31 750,000 5/17 Sch. 52 Forms/C2118/14

Instructions regarding War Diaries and Intelligence Summaries are contained in F. S. Regs., Part II. and the Staff Manual respectively. Title pages will be prepared in manuscript.

DADOS London Div 3

WAR DIARY
or
INTELLIGENCE SUMMARY.
(Erase heading not required.)

September 1919.

Army Form C. 2118.

Place	Date	Hour	Summary of Events and Information	Remarks and references to Appendices
Deutz.	29.		Routine work. returns etc.	
	30		Arranged for 6 lorries to deliver 300 beds etc to 9th East Surrey. Routine work.	

D. D. & L., London, E.C.
(A8004) Wt. W1771/M2 31 750,000 5/17 Sch. 52 Forms/C2118/14

Instructions regarding War Diaries and Intelligence Summaries are contained in F. S. Regs., Part II. and the Staff Manual respectively. Title pages will be prepared in manuscript.

D.A.D.O.S. London Division

WAR DIARY
or
~~INTELLIGENCE SUMMARY.~~
(Erase heading not required.)

October 1919.

Army Form C. 2118.

Place	Date	Hour	Summary of Events and Information	Remarks and references to Appendices
Deutz.	1.		Sent 300 beds etc to 9th E. Surreys. W.O. letter 71/1/6809 (A.2) orders all mats gun wheel to be withdrawn from 4.5" How. batteries & returned to Ordnance. also delete from Mob. Store table. Retn. Med. Trench Mortar Stores to Corps I.C.S. List in triplicate sent ~~A.D.O.S.~~ Instructions to 19th Middx. Routine work. Sent 200 pailliasses to 19th Middx.	
	2.		collect 30 tents from 'C' Battery R.F.A. Overalls.	
	3.		Bulk Indents sent in. routine work. Sent 440 beds to 7th Middx.	
	4.		DAAG called ref. to removal of Army Aux. Horse Coy. from Schools here, the space being required for returned stores, & removal of Heumar dump to Deutz. Routine work.	
	5.		Sunday.	
	6.		Saw ~~A.D.O.S.~~ Routine work.	
	7.		Went G.H.Q. re demand for pailliasses, in connection with BAR letter QA 21/1 d/23/7/19. Routine work.	
	8.		Sent 500 blankets to 10th Queens on loan. G.O.C. wrote VI Corps Q re move of Aux. Horse Coy. from schools next my dump. (Q/4549.)	
	9.		Drawing stores from Nippes depot. Visit to Heumar by S/Cdr Geddes. Routine work.	

D. D. & L., London, E.C. (A8004) Wt. W1771/M2 31 750,000 5/17 Sch. 52 Forms/C2118/14

420

D.A.D.O.S. London Division.

Instructions regarding War Diaries and Intelligence Summaries are contained in F. S. Regs., Part II. and the Staff Manual respectively. Title pages will be prepared in manuscript.

WAR DIARY

or

~~INTELLIGENCE SUMMARY.~~

(Erase heading not required.)

October, 1919

Army Form C. 2118.

Place	Date	Hour	Summary of Events and Information	Remarks and references to Appendices
DEUTZ.	10.	Oct.	Saw Q.M. 9th E. Surreys re their cleansing operations. Applied for 3 lorries to send beds out to 1st Bde. 2 trucks required to clear German dump. That place clean and in good order. Drew stores from Base depot.	
	11.		Routine work. Applied for 10 lorries for Monday for drawing winter clothing from VI Corps. ICS etc.	
	12		Sunday.	
	13		Routine work. Units asked to indent for horse rugs at once. Horse shoes & foot caps not yet available at Base depot. Have now applied there twice.	
	14		Routine work	
	15		Visited A.D.O.S. VI Corps.	
	16		Visited Nos 1 & 2 Coy train & inspected harness. Many bits very much worn & require replacement. Went to Div Q. re return plates & instructions under VI Corps No S.Q. 416. d 13/10/19. Arranged for 20 lorries daily to collect tents etc from units now in billets.	
	17.		10 lorries collecting winter clothing from Cologne Depot.	
	18.		Routine work. Sgt Bolton and 6 RAOC. of my staff demobilised. Ord. Cdr Finch also demobilised.	
	19		Sunday.	

D. D. & L., London, E.C. (A8004) Wt. W1771/M2 31 750,000 5/17 Sch. 52 Forms/C2118/14

DADOS. London Division (3)

Instructions regarding War Diaries and Intelligence Summaries are contained in F. S. Regs., Part II. and the Staff Manual respectively. Title pages will be prepared in manuscript.

WAR DIARY or INTELLIGENCE SUMMARY.

(Erase heading not required.)

October 1919.

Army Form C. 2118.

Place	Date	Hour	Summary of Events and Information	Remarks and references to Appendices
Deutz	20		Routine work. Saw Q Masters 140 F.A. 1/7 Middsx and 2/4 Queens re return of their surplus stores etc. Wrote 3rd Bde. asking if the men who wish to transfer to RAOC & who have been already accepted by ADOS, can be posted to me at once, for preliminary training. 11 of my men having been demobilised during the past few days.	
	21.		'Phoned ADOS (P) re his requirements of requisitioned stores. Beds, mops, safes not required. Visited Div Q re Units difficulties over returning surplus stores etc. Routine work.	
	22		Went to G.H.Q. saw Labour Commandant put in application for 10 Germans to work here until I can replace with British personnel. Confirmed my action re return of stores of doubtful origin to Corps I.C.S. Routine work.	
	23.		Visited Div. Q. re moving my dump. Visited Humboldt Factory re accommodation if I have to move. Went to German salvage dump, also Railhead. Seriously handicapped by lack of men. Saw Baths Officer (St Davis) re 26th R.F. exchange clothing.	
	24		Routine work. Saw Q.M.s re return etc of stores. Visited Merheim reception camp ~~with D.A.Q.M.G.~~ Drawing stores from Cologne Depot.	
	25.		Routine work. No men have arrived yet. Work at Dump considerably handicapped in consequence.	
	26		Sunday.	

D. D. & L., London, E.C. (A10266) Wt W5300/P713 750,000 2/18 Sch. 52 Forms/C2118/16.

D.A.D.O.S.
London Div.

Instructions regarding War Diaries and Intelligence Summaries are contained in F. S. Regs., Part II. and the Staff Manual respectively. Title pages will be prepared in manuscript.

WAR DIARY
or
INTELLIGENCE SUMMARY.
(Erase heading not required.)

October 1919.

(4)

Army Form C. 2118.

Place	Date	Hour	Summary of Events and Information	Remarks and references to Appendices
Deutz	27		Routine work. Arranged with 'Q' to move salvage dump Heumar to the Schools Deutz Freiheit. German labour arrived. Started them loading underclothing for Baths.	
	28.		Moving Heumar salvage dump to Deutz. 7 German civilians started work. 23rd Mdsx Regt. unloaded beds, tables, forms & safes in my yard. These had been sent to VI Corps ICS in error, as the towns were urgently required, I took them in for return to Burgomaster here.	
	29.		Completed moving salvage dump to Deutz-Freiheit School. Deutz Koln. returned Tents & marquees to Corps ICS.	
			Routine work	
	30.		6 men reported from 23rd R.F. for duty, pending exchange to R.A.O.C.	
	31.		Pte Clements sent away for Demob. Visited 'Q' Office re new amendments to Instructions for Disposal of stores. Sent tables & forms etc to Equipment Camp.	

D. D. & L., London, E.C.
(A10266) Wt W5300/P713 750,000 2/18 Sch. 52 Forms/C2118/16.

A. D.A.D.O.S. London Divn. B.A.R.

Instructions regarding War Diaries and Intelligence Summaries are contained in F. S. Regs., Part II. and the Staff Manual respectively. Title pages will be prepared in manuscript.

WAR DIARY
or
INTELLIGENCE SUMMARY.
(Erase heading not required.)

November. 1919.

Army Form C. 2118.

Place	Date	Hour	Summary of Events and Information	Remarks and references to Appendices
DEUTZ Köln.	1.		~~[illegible]~~. Drawing packing cases for Units. 2 men sent to Dispersal camp for demobilisation. Pte Clements & Burns.	
	2.		Sunday.	
	3.		Saw QM. 9th East Surreys re disposal of their stores. routine work.	
	4.		Routine work. Major Commons visited me, ref his taking over DADOS. went to G.H.Q. & confirmed this.	
	5.		Saw O/C 59 San. Sec. received & checked his G1098 & certificates. Saw QM. 19th Middlesex Regt. re rifles & flares.	
	6.		Routine work. Saw 'Q' ref. Units G1098s & Certifs.	
	7.		Visited Merheim Reception Camp, took all the papers G1098 etc of Units who have handed in stores, left them with O/C Camp to be amended according to the alterations in Administrative Instructions. & for inclusion of additional receipts from Corps I.C.S. = 'Q' have issued instructions that all Units must hand completed Certifs & forms to me, & obtain my receipt for same before leaving. Have personally advised the majority of QM's re the correct procedure etc for completing these returns.	
	8		Routine work.	

1577 Wt. W10791/1773 500,000 1/15 D. D. & L. A.D.S.S./Forms/C. 2118.

D.A.D.O.S. London Divn.

Instructions regarding War Diaries and Intelligence Summaries are contained in F. S. Regs., Part II. and the Staff Manual respectively. Title pages will be prepared in manuscript.

WAR DIARY
or
~~INTELLIGENCE SUMMARY~~.
(Erase heading not required.)

November 1919.

Army Form C. 2118.

Place	Date	Hour	Summary of Events and Information	Remarks and references to Appendices
Deutz	9		Sunday.	
	10		Visited Merheim reception camp. taking G1098 various units Divn's for amendment.	
	11		Major L Connors arrived to take over duties as D.A.D.O.S. Large numbers of Indents being received from new Units arriving in this Divn. Handed over to Major L. Connors R.A.O.C. – ~~[illegible]~~	
	12.		Visited A.D.O.S. to consult reference taken over of Garrison. also saw 'Q'	
	13			
	14		Q.Ws of 1st Rhine Garrison Bde interviewed re further supplies of winter clothing	
	15		Routine work	
	16		Sunday	
	17		Inspected and conditioned surplus stores for return to Base	
	18		Interviewed late Commanders of 1, 2, 3 Sections London DAC in connection with documents required on disbandment of Units	

DADOS Rhine Garrison

Instructions regarding War Diaries and Intelligence Summaries are contained in F. S. Regs., Part II. and the Staff Manual respectively. Title pages will be prepared in manuscript.

WAR DIARY
or
INTELLIGENCE SUMMARY.
(Erase heading not required.)

November 19

Army Form C. 2118.

Place	Date	Hour	Summary of Events and Information	Remarks and references to Appendices
Deutz	19		Drew up schedule of equipment required for Officers Messes and Quarters. Routine work	
	20th		Visited 140 and 142 Field Ambulances 52 Mobile Vet. Section No. 2 Section Garrison Train. Ordnance situation satisfactory 140 Field Ambulance require vehicles to be overhauled Arranged	
	21st		Visited 41 M.G.C. Satisfactory. 51st Rifle Brigade, Require a large quantity of cleaning material for barrack rooms supply arranged, also need a quantity of wagon equipment Unit instructed to demand. 52nd Rifle Brigade. Require cooks clothing. Arranged. All vehicles require inspection. Arranged for I.O.M. to attend. 23rd Royal Fusiliers wheels of vehicles require working up. Indent arranged.	
	22nd		Routine work	
	23rd		Sunday	

DADOS

Rhine Garrison

WAR DIARY
or
INTELLIGENCE SUMMARY.
(Erase heading not required.)

November 19

Army Form C. 2118.

Instructions regarding War Diaries and Intelligence Summaries are contained in F. S. Regs., Part II. and the Staff Manual respectively. Title pages will be prepared in manuscript.

Place	Date	Hour	Summary of Events and Information	Remarks and references to Appendices
Deutz	24th		Conference at Garrison HQ attended by all staff Captains & QMs 11th Queens Regt want caps supply arranged	
	25th		QM Inniskilling Dragoons called reference supply of crockery for officers mess. Instructed to demand.	
	26th		Visited ADOS Corps, Corps IOO & OO Corps Troops & obtained a quantity of saddlery and cleaning material	
	27th		Inspected & conditioned stores for Base	
	28th		Visited 18th Brigade RFA & comprising batteries. Issue of horse rugs not completed, expedited "A" Battery harness & vehicles require examination. Attended to	
	29th		Routine work	
	30		Sunday	

Gordon Major
DADOS RG
30/11/19

1577 Wt. W10791/1773 500,000 1/15 D. D. & L. A.D.S.S./Forms/C. 2118.

www.ingramcontent.com/pod-product-compliance
Lightning Source LLC
Chambersburg PA
CBHW081245170426
43191CB00034B/2042

* 9 7 8 1 4 7 4 5 1 9 9 8 4 *